The World According to Bill O'Reilly

Other Books by Ken Lawrence

The World According to Michael Moore
The World According to Trump
The World According to Oprah

THE WORLD
ACCORDING TO
BILL O'REILLY

An Unauthorized Portrait in His Own Words

KEN LAWRENCE

**Andrews McMeel
Publishing**

Kansas City

05 06 07 08 09 MLT 10 9 8 7 6 5 4 3 2 1

Library of Congress Cataloging-in-Publication Data

O'Reilly, Bill.
    The world according to Bill O'Reilly : an unauthorized
portrait in his own words / [compiled by] Ken Lawrence.
        p.   cm.
    ISBN-13: 978-0-7407-5478-4
    ISBN-10: 0-7407-5478-5
    1. O'Reilly, Bill—Quotations. I. Lawrence, Ken. II. Title.
PN4874.O73A25   2005
791.4502'8'092—dc22

                                    2005048005

Design by Kelly & Company, Lee's Summit, Missouri

www.andrewsmcmeel.com

Contents

Introduction

Love him or hate him, hero or huckster, one thing is for sure: Bill O'Reilly refuses to be ignored.

With the highest-rated cable TV news program, O'Reilly's in-your-face style of interviewing has given him a popular platform to skewer his opponents and right the wrongs he sees around him. No doubt about it, O'Reilly is an angry man. "I'm angry about a number of things. Centrally, that the people who make this country work, the millions of people that get up at six in the morning, get home at six at night, don't have a lot of power. And the people that they give power to represent them, more often than not, sell them out. That really tees me off."

O'Reilly traces his indignation to his roots on Long Island, New York, where he says he ran with a tough crowd. "You had to be strong and feisty. If you weren't, life was not easy." He also says that listening to his father's deathbed pronouncement that he "didn't fulfill [his] potential" steeled his resolve to help working-class people like himself who get stomped by what he perceives as a system stacked against them.

O'Reilly was raised in a traditional Roman Catholic setting and went to Catholic school. As a teenager, he mowed lawns and eventually established a house-painting business. This instilled his strong work ethic, which continues today.

He graduated from Marist College in Poughkeepsie, New York, with a degree in history and taught high school for two years in Miami, Florida. O'Reilly then attended Boston University where he received a master's in broadcast journalism.

In 1975, he got a job as a reporter for WNEP-TV in Scranton, Pennsylvania, making $150 a week. In 1980, he anchored a show for WCBS-TV in New York and, later, he became a correspondent for CBS News and covered wars in El Salvador and the Falkland Islands.

Bill O'Reilly joined ABC News as a correspondent on ABC's *World News Tonight* in 1986. During his three-year tenure, he appeared on the show more than one hundred times, and received two Emmy Awards and two National Headliner Awards for excellence in reporting.

In 1989, O'Reilly replaced David Frost as host of *Inside Edition,* one of the earliest "infotainment" shows that combined traditional journalism with edgy comment, opinion, and titillation. "In all fairness," wrote *Chicago Tribune* television critic Clifford Terry at the time, "*Inside Edition* is more tawdry than trashy." With O'Reilly as anchor, the show soared in ratings against similar programs like *A Current Affair,* and O'Reilly's aggressive on-air persona became more pronounced and popular.

O'Reilly decided to leave behind a reported million dollar a year salary in 1995 to attend the John F. Kennedy School of Government and earned a master's degree in public policy. He wrote a novel titled *Those Who Trespass* about the broadcast TV business. In it, the lead character, a TV anchor, gets fired because his enemies rig a survey to show he's losing popularity. "He's out to get the people who rigged the research," O'Reilly says of the thriller.

Although the book enjoyed modest success, his next move was the big one. He took a job in October 1996 as anchor of *The O'Reilly Report,* which later became *The O'Reilly Factor,* on then-upstart Fox News Channel. TV has never been the same since.

What followed was a torrent of O'Reilly offerings, including books (*The O'Reilly Factor, The No Spin Zone, Who's Looking Out for You?* and one for teens titled *The O'Reilly Factor for Kids*), a syndicated radio show called *The Radio Factor,* and a syndicated column carried in newspapers across the country.

With these successes came some tough times. In 2004, an associate producer threatened O'Reilly with a harassment suit, claiming that he directed inappropriate sexual behavior and lewd remarks toward her. O'Reilly's lawyers charged that the woman was trying to extort money from the TV star. The two parties settled out of court with O'Reilly paying the woman an undisclosed amount reportedly in the millions of dollars. Speaking publicly about the matter, O'Reilly told his fans on the show: "All litigation has ceased in the case that has made me the object of media scorn from coast to coast. Today, lawyers issued a statement saying there was no wrong-doing in the case whatsoever by anyone." The popular O'Reilly bounced back from this incident without missing a step and he continues to tilt at windmills.

For all his success, O'Reilly claims to be an everyday regular guy, still living on Long Island with his wife and two daughters and hanging out with his childhood pals. "They're still my friends—first grade, kindergarten. I still keep in touch with those guys."

Here then, in his own words, are comments from someone who may be a regular guy, but who certainly is not ordinary.

On
Celebrities
and
Hollywood

My latest jihad
was to go after the
Hollywood celebrities.

—*Kansas City Star,* November 13, 2001,
citing a speech at a local Red Cross fund-raiser

You know, I think the genesis of this is that Hollywood has been pretty much given a free pass forever by the television media. Very rarely have they been criticized. . . . Now they know that that protection will never be afforded them ever again because what we do here is we watch the powerful and the famous and if they misbehave we report on it. . . . No one is safe from our scrutiny.

—*New York Post,* January 3, 2002

All I said to the movie stars was, "Look, if you're going to go on a telethon and look at the camera and say 100 percent of all this money is going to go to the families, then you'd better damn well make sure that that happens." They didn't like that. . . . I respect George Clooney. I think he's a well-intentioned guy. But like so many people, he doesn't think things out. And his ego overrides his mind. These stars all have a sense of entitlement. They think they're entitled not to be criticized.

—*Dallas Morning News,* February 17, 2002

On
Children

What is your idea of perfect happiness?

Seeing little kids having a great time.

—*Vanity Fair,* March 2003

What kind of father are you?

I was a teacher. I apply the lessons I learned from that more than I could from the home I grew up in, because it isn't the same country that I grew up in. You've got to know what the hell is going on. Because if you don't, by the time your kid is nine, he's going to have all kinds of values that you're going to be horrified by. So you'd better know what that kid's doing, what he's looking at, and what he's hearing.

—*Time* magazine, October 6, 2003

It's never been harder to be a child. When you and I were growing up— and you're a lot older than I am—it was much different. And we were exposed to the horrors of the world about twelve, thirteen, fourteen in the school yard and on like that. Now they're exposed to them seven, eight, and nine because of the machines: the media, the computers, shock radio, and cable and all of this. So children very, very young get bombarded with stuff that they can't possibly process and

they are confused. Now that's number
one. It's the hardest part of our history
to be a child. Number two, the way to
solve at least partially that problem for
parents is to talk to their kids. Every
research shows if you talk to your
children you've got a better chance
of keeping them out of rehab and
keeping them out of the penitentiary.

—*Today,* October 7, 2004

On the Clintons

Bush sees the office as a form
of responsibility. Clinton got in
office with cigars and said,
"Let the good times roll."

—*Morning Call* (Allentown, Pennsylvania),
January 5, 2003, citing a speech at
a fund-raiser for Easton Theater

A guy [Bill Clinton] like that
to become president of the United
States—it's another Abe Lincoln.
[He comes] from nowhere, gets
elected to the highest office in the
world; how did this happen? . . .
Clinton's mindset is, "There really
isn't a right and a wrong. I don't
make those kinds of judgments;
I see both sides."

❖⟵≡◉≡⟶❖

—*Daily Free Press,* April 2, 2002,
citing a speech at Boston University

She [Senator Hillary Clinton] was talking to a blue-collar crowd. She doesn't connect with those people and never has.

—*New York Daily News,* October 24, 2001

It [his unsuccessful bid to outsell Senator Hillary Clinton's book] was just for sport. We wanted to see if we could beat her. Everyone loves a horse race.

—*Fort Worth Star-Telegram,* February 10, 2004

The prosecutor, [Kenneth] Starr, and the boys and Robert Ray, were never really able to articulate to the American public what this [Whitewater investigation] was all about. They couldn't explain it, and the press really couldn't explain it, unless they were reading very, very intricately into the *New York Times* or the *Washington Post*. So 95 percent of the American people never got what this was all about, and therefore didn't care. Ray and Starr had an obligation to engage the public and explain not only what the investigation was, but why it was taking place. They never did it . . . it was ridiculous. Why did they spend all this money? What did they find out?

—*Talk of the Nation,* September 21, 2000

On
George
W. Bush

Bush knows that people are voting hope on both sides. And so the president is going to put out that he's optimistic of victory. So that's the hope to vote for President Bush. John Kerry wants you to hope that he's going to be able to persuade other nations to help us in Iraq to stabilize the situation. So, both—both candidates—are asking you to make a leap of faith on their behalf. And so, it isn't as difficult as you might think it would be. Bush is going to stay on one track: We're going to prevail, we're going to win. And that's what he's going to say no matter what you ask him.

—*Good Morning America,* September 28, 2004

I think Bush is pandering to the electorate by a whole bunch of programs. And you know that the No Child Left Behind Act and all the federal money that poured in to try to help the kids, which, you know, everybody wants to help the kids—Right?—states can't spend the money. Most of the states are going to have to give it back to the Treasury because they just can't spend the money. They're not organized enough.

-→≡◎≡←-

—Interview with Bill O'Reilly and Paul Krugman
by Tim Russert, cited by *Philadelphia
Inquirer,* September 24, 2004

And I said on my program if, if the Americans go in and overthrow Saddam Hussein and it's clean, he has nothing [weapons of mass destruction], I will apologize to the nation and I will not trust the Bush administration again.

All right? But I'm giving my government the benefit of the doubt.

—*Good Morning America,* February 10, 2004

Bush people fear me, because if I turn on Bush, that's 10 million people a day that are hearing that, and they [the Bush people] don't want that.

—*Palm Beach Post* (Florida), February 2, 2004

All people are going to make mistakes. I would rather have a guy say "bring them on" than some stiff guy with no emotion. They like him because he reacted the way they did right after 9/11. That's why they like him. That was a bonding, right? And that will never go away. However, people want performance. You've got to stabilize the economy, you've got to explain weapons of mass destruction, and stop the killing in Iraq. You have to. But remember, the Democrats really haven't mounted any kind of momentum here so we're all waiting to see if Hillary Clinton jumps in. Because none of the Democrats right now have broken out of the pack.

—*Good Morning America,* July 30, 2003

I don't think there's any doubt about that George W. Bush wanted to remove Saddam. And in history, I believe that will be a good thing. . . . But I think every American should be very concerned, for their families and themselves, that our intelligence isn't as good as it should be.

—Associated Press, February 12, 2004, citing ABC's *Good Morning America*

On
Inside
Edition

People *feel* when they watch us. People want that. When you invest time to read a book, you want to feel something. The same is true if you're watching television. We believe in advocacy journalism.

—*Chicago Tribune,* August 30, 1991

We take a sharp point of view.
We say, "He's a rat, and he's a victim."
We've refined the emotional approach to
stories. The networks are picking up on
it. I hope network news never becomes
more like *Inside Edition*. But they are.

—*Orlando Sentinel,* August 26, 1991

That's what drives our show *[Inside Edition]*: emotion. All of our stories are emotion-driven. If they don't have emotion, we don't do 'em. That emotion has changed the way the viewer looks at the news. And the viewer doesn't understand it. . . . If you watch *Inside Edition* and then you turn on *Nightline*, and there's no emotion in *Nightline* at all, and there's all this emotion in *Inside Edition*, you're going, "There's something missing here! . . ."

—Associated Press, December 18, 1992

I've tried very hard to represent the broadcast with honesty and integrity. I hope I have succeeded. . . . Read up on O. J. Simpson.

—Associated Press, October 24, 1994,
on leaving the show and giving advice
to his replacement, Deborah Norville

On the
Iraq War

Look, the Iraq War was a big screw-up, all right? I think every clear-thinking person in the country knows it was. First of all, weapons of mass destruction did not materialize, which was the primary motivator for the war.

—*Tim Russert*, CNBC, August 14, 2004

I don't want one soldier dying for them. . . . They don't appreciate us. . . . The faster we get out of there, the better. We gave them a chance like we gave the South Vietnamese people a chance."

—*South Bend Tribune* (Indiana), May 24, 2004, citing a speech at Lake Michigan College

You think they think rationally? They don't. These are fanatics. This is what everybody has to understand. You can't reason with these people, all right? There's always an excuse. There's always a way. They want to kill Americans. They're going to try to kill Americans. They don't care whether this guy [Saddam Hussein] was pulled out of the dirt or not. Thank God there aren't that many of them, and now the cowards who run them will start to run like rats. So I expect things to improve.

—*Today,* December 15, 2003

If you [filmmaker Michael Moore] were running the country, [Saddam Hussein] would still be sitting there.

—*New York Sun,* July 28, 2004

On Senator
John Kerry

I think Kerry's an honest guy.
You ask him a question, and
he tells you what he thinks.
He's not a weasel. I just hope
he's calling the shots
in his campaign.

—Associated Press, October 7, 2004

I've known Kerry for twenty-five years. He's a patriot. I'm listening to what he has to say.

—*60 Minutes,* cited by *Edmonton Journal* (Alberta), September 25, 2004

On the
Media

There's no question
[National Public Radio is]
a left-wing outfit.

—*Philadelphia Daily News,*
October 21, 2003

I submit to you that because we have twenty-four-hour, round-the-clock news, we have news on the Internet, we have news on the radio, that the American public is much better informed and scoundrels are least likely to get away with stuff than in the past.

—*The NewsHour with Jim Lehrer,*
November 13, 1998

It's a pack mentality, because the original thinkers, the creative journalists, have been weeded out, and what you got is yes-men now. "Yes, yes, yes." So they don't have an idea in their brain. They just see what everybody else is doing so they all run after Monica Lewinsky. "There she is. Let's go get Monica! Oh, there's William Ginsburg. Let's go get him." Is there any thought put into it? No, because the thinkers have been assassinated by the people at the top of television news who fear them.

⊷⊜⊷

—The Osgood File, July 10, 1998

One of the things that I say in [the book] *Who's Looking Out for You?* is that the media isn't looking out for you. They don't care about you. They don't know who you are and they don't want to know who you are.

—*The Big Story with John Gibson,* November 5, 2003

I despise journalists and media people. I despise those who try to ram an ideology down your throat saying, I know better than you. And you should listen to me. And if you don't listen to me I'm going to twist it around. I hate that. We're the—we're the watchdogs here. And we watch the media. And, you know, I can't be part of the elite media and watch them.

—*The Big Story Weekend Edition,* September 27, 2003

I do respect you [*USA Today* columnist who said O'Reilly had bad on-camera manners] for coming in here and taking the heat. Most weasels in your category wouldn't have.

—United Press International, July 9, 2003

The traditional way of covering news is over. If I were running a network, I'd get that message loud and clear.

—*New York Daily News,* May 8, 2003

When I was growing up, I didn't care about the news at all. I had no interest in the news. But my father liked you. No spin. . . . And I said, "That guy, he's pretty interesting because he's giving people a hard time." Which is what you did. So then, when I got older, there were three guys that I watched: you, Howard Cosell . . . and Tom Snyder, because Snyder knew how to work that camera. You were the three. So you're responsible.

—Talking to Dan Rather, CBSNews.com,
September 26, 2004

And another thing I want to yell at you guys about is the way every time you write about me, you put a little pejorative adjective in front of my name. "The conservative Bill O'Reilly." In the *Boston Globe* the other day, it was, "The conservative hatchet man." Or "bellicose." It's always a pejorative.

—*St. Paul Pioneer Press,* January 28, 2002

There's no bitterness to a journalist's anger. If you're not teed off about problems in our society, you have no business being a journalist. The profession was set up to challenge the ills of our society and the mistakes of those in power.

—ABCNEWS.com, Friday, November 9, 2001

The problem with television news in the year 2000 is that it's no longer necessary. The network chiefs don't understand that. . . . It's over for the Establishment, that's for sure. It's like the last days of Pompeii. . . . The networks' philosophy is that we're going to decide what information is important. At Fox News Channel, we're not going do that. We're going to give you all sides.

⟿⟾

—*Boston Globe,* September 28, 2000

I'm in the vanguard on television of our search and destroy mission about the elite media. And I'm proud of the fact that we have taken these people down— not on a personal level—but on a level that's going to open up communications and information to all Americans.

—FreeRepublic.com, May 20, 2001, citing a speech at *Talkers Magazine*'s New Media Seminar

What I wanted to do was bring unfiltered information into your homes. I'm basically a problem-solver. . . . I'm not understanding why the networks are doing what they're doing. They want to do what they want to do. Fine. I'm crushing them [in the ratings].

—*Arkansas Democrat-Gazette* (Little Rock), June 18, 2000, citing a speech and later comments at a Republican fund-raiser

On
Money

There's a lot of money at stake here. It's always about money in television news. It's always about money. It's never about the work. The work comes second.

—*Times-Picayune* (New Orleans, Louisiana), January 21, 2002

Class is a sensibility. You don't have to sell out, you don't have to be one of the swells, just because you have a lot of money. I have a nice house. I drive a good car, though it's not a luxury model. And that's it. I'm not really into materialism.

—*Miami Herald,* July 7, 2003

I don't care about money. The frightening thing is that I don't—I'm not a materialist. You know, I just live the same way that I always lived. I have a nice house. I provide for the people in my family, but that's it. I don't zip around in a Ferrari and hang in at Le Cirque. I'm not doing that, you know? I mean, I'm eating at the same diner I always ate at. So that's me. But it's nice to have the security, and it's nice to be able to help people with the jack.

—*Tim Russert,* CNBC, October 4, 2003

I have held some tech stocks that got battered. . . . I believe in technology. I still have stock in companies like EMC. I think they'll come back. But I have been wrong a lot. So don't take my advice.

—*New York Times,* August 18, 2002

I will not go in a Starbucks.

—*Newsweek,* February 12, 2001

On
The No Spin Zone

Well, you know, it's interesting, because this—*The No Spin Zone* book, the reason that it's selling so well, is because it's basically good versus evil in the book.

—*Your World with Neil Cavuto,*
October 24, 2001

Now what I can't understand is, number one, the appeasers [of evil]. And there are only maybe 12 percent of Americans are like that; 88 percent understand what we're up against. And number two, why Americans have such a hard time in general accepting evil, and that's the theme of *The No Spin Zone* book: that evil can hide behind the First Amendment; it can hide behind political correctness and that Americans have a very hard time with it because we haven't seen it since World War II.

⋅◆══◉══◆⋅

—*Tim Russert,* CNBC, December 29, 2001

On
The O'Reilly
Factor TV
Show

It's a battle of wits. Who's the quicker draw intellectually. I enjoy the joust. And I think people enjoy watching the joust and that's one of the reasons we're real successful.

—*60 Minutes,* September 26, 2004

The show's taken on a different kind of cachet. People know if they want to get their message out to a vast audience that they need to do this. . . . You have to engage people now. What they want is strong opinions about the news they already know. They don't need a feature about people making candy canes in Wisconsin. You guys [the network news shows] are old-fashioned dinosaurs. You guys are petrified forests.

—*Dallas Morning News,* September 3, 2004

The show was a little softer
in the beginning than it is now.
We kind of did 50–50 hard news
and features, because at six o'clock
your audience is a little bit older.

—*Los Angeles Times,* May 2, 2004

My job is to expose people for who they are.

—*The Early Show,* October 3, 2003

We don't allow BS, and I call
people on it. But it's not like
I call them names.

—*Fort Worth Star-Telegram*,
July 17, 2003

I always knew news analysis would work in prime time. We just had to give it time.

—*Miami Herald,* July 10, 2003

I'm in the arena every day. I'm a gunslinger. Every day I deal with people I think are hurting the country in one way or another. Every local market I was ever in as a reporter, I righted wrongs in those markets. I brought bad guys down, brought them down hard. If you're not in it to expose corruption, to make the bad guys tremble, get out.

—*Times-Picayune* (New Orleans, Louisiana), May 17, 2003

Every time we put [the Laci Peterson] story on, the ratings spike. It's the only thing keeping Larry King on the air. We do Laci Peterson every fifteen minutes and see the numbers go up. It's a story that resonates with women particularly.

—*Vanity Fair,* August 2003

We're the first prime-time news program to analyze events from the workingman's point of view. We have no agenda. We're not trying to get anyone elected. We're just trying to help regular people make sense of the world.

—*Entertainment Weekly,* December 21, 2001

It's very intense, there is opinion that flies back and forth, and whoever has the stronger argument wins. We don't have any agenda. We don't serve an ideology. And we keep an eye on the powerful. It's a populist program. . . .

—*Sun Herald* (Biloxi, Mississippi), March 1, 2001

Each segment's like a racing car going around the track. Is this O'Reilly going to beat this guy, or this guy going to beat O'Reilly? It's an intellectual joust, and that's the way I designed the show. I wanted it to be like the old Mike Wallace *Nightbeat* in the fifties, with a contemporary twist. I'm not looking to be obnoxious, but I am going to challenge everything.

—*Record* (Kitchener-Waterloo, Ontario),
March 11, 1999

We got more people wanting to come on the show than we could possibly book. They like the intellectual joust, and even if they lose, they get credit for coming on. Especially the men: They're macho guys, so if they're single, they get more dates.

—*New York Observer,* April 9, 2001

Our opinions are pretty well researched and they're backed by fact. Some people like them, some people don't.

—*Desert Sun* (Palm Springs, California),
March 7, 2003

On
The O'Reilly
Factor Book

This book is huge. How come I'm not on *Good Morning America* and the *Today* show? Am I boring? I got Random House behind me, the biggest publishing house in the world, pitching me over there, and they're, like, "We'll pass." Where's Oprah's book club? I'm writing this book for working-class Americans, which is what watches her program. How come I'm not sitting next to Oprah? I'll give her a big kiss and I'll bring brownies.

—*Newsday* (New York), October 18, 2000

Well, I wasn't really elite. I mean, believe me. I was sub-elite, but I worked for you guys. But I've been having trouble getting on a lot of the big shows with this book. . . .

—*Good Morning America,* October 10, 2000

On His
Personal Life

All litigation has ceased in the case [sexual harassment lawsuit] that has made me the object of media scorn from coast to coast. Today, lawyers issued a statement saying there was no wrongdoing in the case whatsoever by anyone. Obviously, the words "no wrongdoing" are the key. On a personal note, this matter has caused enormous pain, but I had to protect my family and I did. Some of the media hammered me relentlessly because, as you know, I'm a huge target, as is Fox News. This brutal ordeal is now officially over and I will never speak of it again.

—*Good Morning America,* October 29, 2004

They can throw anything they
want at me, I'll take it, and in the
end, we'll see who's left standing.

—*NBC Nightly News,* October 28, 2004

I'll always be interested in exposing this mentality among certain people in positions of power that says, "I'm above the law and don't have to be accountable the way average Americans do."

—*American Enterprise,* March 1, 2001

I don't eat a lot of food anyway. I do eat grapefruits when I'm on the run, and I'll have like a power shake, but I don't really have time to eat. I work out in the morning, do push-ups and sit-ups and try to take a thirty-minute walk every day. I try to zip out of the building, wearing shades and maybe a jacket, and I walk through Rockefeller Center, I walk around Broadway or whatever, and I walk fast. Because I'm six four, people don't perceive that. I don't get mobbed in the sense that people are intrusive. But I've got to move fast.

⊰══◆══⊱

—Cox News Service, February 1, 2004

The essence of Long Island is that back then you were thrown out as a little kid five, six, seven years old into an unsupervised soup of diversity where you had Italians, Jews, Irish, Polish kids—everybody running around, and you had to be strong and feisty. If you weren't, life was not easy.

—*Newsday* (New York), December 7, 2003

I'm not going to live in Manhattan. I mean, you know, I want a tree once in a while. Just, you know, let me see a normal—this is a concrete jungle here, and while I respect the city and know the city as well as anyone on earth, I think, I want to have a little breathing room, so I do live out in the burbs.

—*Tim Russert,* CNBC, May 24, 2003

Anybody who knows me will tell you I've been the same way for thirty years. I mean, I was the same way when I got a letter from my third-grade teacher, Sister Mary Lorana, and she goes, "You have the same expression you had back then." I'm the same guy. It's not an act.

—Topic A with Tina Brown, April 30, 2003

I keep religion fairly private. I'm a traditional Roman Catholic. I go to church. I think that everybody should keep their sex lives and religion private. Now, you can talk about it with somebody in the sense of a question. You can explain to them, "Well here's what I believe and why I believe it," but I'm not somebody who is going around to your door trying to sell you a pamphlet.

—*Saturday Evening Post,* January 1, 2003

I'm angry about a number of things, centrally, that the people who make this country work, the millions of people that get up at six in the morning, get home at six at night, don't have a lot of power. And the people that they give power to represent them, more often than not, sell them out. That really tees me off.

—*Primetime Thursday,* November 8, 2001

In this month's *Cigar Aficionado* magazine . . . the last page, there's an article about me and my friends, the guys that I grew up with. They're still my friends—first grade, kindergarten. I still keep in touch with those guys.

And I believe that every American should have a support system outside of their job and their marriage because those things—I hate to say it—I think come and go. But true friends will stay forever. And you have to have people that you can go to and talk about things and people who can be honest with you and say, "Hey, listen, O'Reilly, you're a lunatic. Shut up once in a while. Listen to the guest." Those kinds of people.

—*The Edge with Paula Zahn,* September 14, 2000

Fifteen years ago, my father was on his deathbed, and he said to me, "My one regret in life is that I didn't fulfill my potential." He was born in Brooklyn, he went to Lincoln High School, his father was a cop and [he] was an accountant. He bought into the system, and the system didn't treat him well. I decided that if I ever reached a position of prominence in this country, that I would write a book that told working-class people what the rules of the game really are, not the myths that the elite media throw at you.

⋅→═◉═←⋅

—*San Diego Union-Tribune,* December 16, 2000

On
Politics and
Politicians

Every politician is self-serving in every party. So if it's going to help them, they're going to do it; if it's going to hurt them they won't.

—*Today,* March 11, 2004

Shark, sure, fine. Just call me
a shark, I'm happy. Sharks will be mad,
I'm happy. Ultraconservative? Absurd.

—Canadian Press, May 2, 2004

Yeah, maybe he could mobilize a certain number of independent thinkers who think, "This guy could be a . . . Teddy Roosevelt kind of guy, who could come in and clean up the garbage . . ." but I'm not a vanity player, I'm not going to go out like Al Sharpton, to get on *Saturday Night Live* to run for president, so unless I'm convinced I could pull it off [a successful political campaign], I wouldn't do it.

—*Newsday* (New York), November 13, 2003

I think if I ever did run for office that I would not wage a traditional campaign. I would conduct myself not as a politician, but as an American citizen.

—*Boston Globe,* October 24, 1989

Obviously I don't want any leader to be someone we can't trust. I think what we have, though, is a climate now, in—not only in politics, but also in the media, where people think that they can get away with saying anything. See, I don't think Al Gore gets up every day and goes, I'm going to sell three lies. I don't think he does that.

—*Hannity & Colmes,* September 28, 2000

There comes a point when all of us as Americans have to trust the government until they violate our trust.

—*Desert Sun* (Palm Springs, California), March 9, 2003, citing the third Desert Town Hall Indian Wells speaker series

I think it's important that you come up with more creative questions and more pointed questions.

—Speaking about the 2000 presidential debates, the Associated Press, October 18, 2000

On Ronald Reagan's Death

People want to feel good about their country, and they did in the eighties, particularly in the mid-eighties when Ronald Reagan was at his apex and the country was cooking economically, and then after he left office when the Berlin Wall came down and America was perceived to be the liberator of hundreds of thousands of people. And all of those things are remembered.

And now we're in a kind of a difficult time with the war on terrorism and a lot of polarization inside the United States. So any kind of nostalgia just sixteen years ago is going to have a tremendous appeal for people, and that's what I think you're seeing here.

—*Today,* June 10, 2004

On
Terrorism

We have an obligation to protect our citizens here. If we can get a coalition, fine. But we don't have to get a coalition. And to say we're not going to do anything until such and such a nation gives us an OK is insane. Can you put yourself in a position if somebody just lost their wife, daughter, son, or husband, and we're going to wait until a foreign nation gives us the OK? It's crazy.

—*Good Morning America*, October 3, 2001

We haven't made the adjustment to evil. We hear President Bush say, "Oh, the evildoers," and he's mocked in some circles. . . . It isn't oversimplifying. They are evil people. They don't want to replace us with anything, they don't want to make the world better, they want to destroy things. So how do you deal with that? You have to destroy them by whatever means necessary. And unless Americans understand that they're going to have to have a sacrifice, they're going to have to overcome their personal fear, we won't win that war.

—*Good Morning America,* October 23, 2001

They can't justify this guy [Sami Al-Arian]. He's sitting in Florida; he's getting paid by the taxpayers, and he's got terrorist ties. That's a big story.

—*University Wire,* October 5, 2001

On Those
Who Trespass

When I wrote this book—this is the first novel I've ever written, and I didn't know whether it was good at all. And I'm pounding away at it. You know how the publishing industry is. Everything's terrible, so I just decided to give it to a selected few people. You [Catherine Crier] were one of them because, number one, you work in the industry, and number two, you told me at one time you liked murder mysteries. So I figured, "Well, if she likes this, then maybe it's decent."

And then I had to read you to see—
because you're a nice person, unlike
me, who says—you know, if it's no
good, I'll say, "Oh, it's no good." But
you'd say, "Oh, it was"—you know. . . .
But then I had to kind of read it,
but you liked it and it was just that
really helped me in this process.

—*The Crier Report,* March 30, 1998

The *Hollywood Reporter* said the other day that some execs at King World . . . are nervous that O'Reilly's novel will make them look dreadful. Untrue. Sure, it's a thinly veiled novel about TV news, local and network, but it's not about anybody I've ever worked with. Then what is it about? It's kind of like a [Michael] Crichton book—inside TV in thriller form. The lead character is a TV anchor who gets fired because his enemies rig a survey to show he's losing popularity. He's out to get the people who rigged the research.

—*Newsday* (New York), February 3, 1995

On *Who's Looking Out* for You?

It's not conservative. It has conservative principles. It has liberal principles. This is about trying to help people.

—Associated Press, November 9, 2003

I probably mention the book too many times, and I don't want to be a huckster, but I just feel so strongly that if you read what I'm giving you here with *Who's Looking Out for You?* that it will help you. I mean it's a compilation of my experiences over thirty years, and it's basically don't do what I did, don't be an idiot like I was.

—*On the Record with Greta Van Susteren,*
October 6, 2003

It's divided into three areas. It's the personal, because if you don't know who is looking out for you your life's gonna be bad. All right? You're going to be in divorce court, custody battles over children, you're gonna be bankrupt and all of that. So, you gotta know personally who's looking out for you. And you've gotta be able to read people. You gotta be able to know who they are, whether they're good or bad, whether they care about you or they don't. So, there's a large part of the book.

—*Good Morning America,* September 23, 2003

The book is called *Who's Looking Out for You?* as you know, all right? And you got to look out for yourself is one of the main themes of the book. And if you're going to abuse any part of yourself, whether it's physical or mental or emotional, I'm going to tell you, "Try not to do that" because I want your life to be good. This book is not about me, it's about you.

—*Dateline NBC,* September 21, 2003

Miscellaneous Thoughts

I would decriminalize marijuana, but you step out of your house high and you bother somebody else in any way, shape, or form, I'm going to slap a fine on you that's going to curl your hair!

—*New York Observer,* October 9, 2000

Yesterday on the floor of Congress, Matt, they mentioned O'Reilly as being the driving force. We're not giving up on this. We're going to get that money. We're going to shake it out of those charities, and we're going to make sure it gets to those families [victims of the 9/11 attack], where Americans want it to be. We're on the side of the angels here. George Clooney is misinformed—all right?—and so is Tom Hanks. They should be right with me standing there saying, "Get the money to the people."

—*Today,* November 9, 2001

And you don't take the race element out of the discussion, but what I'm saying to you is that the opportunity in this country exists for all races now. We're beyond trying to put you down because you're a color. We're beyond that here. Sure, if you're a certain color in a certain place or a certain religion in a certain place, you're going to get harassed. That's indisputable. But in the overall picture of America today, the opportunity exists

for everyone. However, it breaks down
on how much opportunity. And for the
working class, whether you're black,
you're white, you're yellow, you're red—
doesn't matter—you're not as great as
the other people who have inherited
money and who have connections.

—*The Early Show,* March 6, 2001

I don't have any problem with NPR or Terry Gross. I do have a problem with [tax dollars] paying for propaganda.

—*Philadelphia Inquirer,* October 14, 2003

By recording snippets or samples of President Bush's speeches and blatantly distorting them out of context merely to serve their own anti-American agenda, these music terrorists [certain hip-hop artists] take the misinformed liberal left to new lows.

—*San Francisco Chronicle*, November 6, 2003

I like people who are in the middle. They understand the world but don't allow it to paralyze them.

—*Harvard Crimson,* April 2, 2002, citing a speech at the Kennedy School of Government's ARCO Forum

It's not a political jihad. Instead of answering the questions and coming clean about his organization, Jesse Jackson wants you to think he's being persecuted.

—*Weekend Edition Saturday,* April 7, 2001

If Fox News is a conservative channel—and I'm going to use the word "if"—so what? You've got fifty other media that are blatantly left. Now, I don't think Fox is a conservative channel. I think it's a traditional channel. There's a difference. We are willing to hear points of view that you'll never hear on ABC, CBS, or NBC.

—*USA Today,* September 2, 2004

They [Al Franken and others] can't win the debate. They can't win the ratings war. So let's turn to defamation and we'll hide behind the satirist's label to defame.

—*Washington Post,* June 27, 2004

I got nothing against the Canadian people, but in the last few years you've swung dramatically to the left. And we in America have some questions about that.

—*Portage Daily Graphic* (Manitoba, Canada), May 3, 2004

What Other People Say About Bill O'Reilly

There's been a lot of back and forth between the two of us and this is just a good way to clear the air.

—Al Franken challenging Bill O'Reilly to a game of bowling to decide the winner of their ongoing feud in the *Aberdeen American News* (South Dakota), October 1, 2004

Were you [*Daily Show* host Jon Stewart] offended when Bill O'Reilly called your viewers "stoned slackers"?

I didn't realize it. Listen, I never watch my show. I don't care for it. So I was excited just to know who was watching.

—Jon Stewart in the *Chicago Sun-Times*,
September 30, 2004

O'Reilly's combativeness and array of rhetorical gambits make getting a word in edgewise nearly impossible for guests on his show, let alone beating him. If O'Reilly wants to take you out early in an interview, he'll narrow his eyes in that Clint Eastwood–style what-kinda-nut-are-you squint that he has. The hands go up in the air as his eyes roll, or the two fingers come up and fire at the camera lenses like a pair of six-shooters. The *O'Reilly Factor* production assistants are already carrying your KO'd body off the set, and Bill has yet to open his mouth.

—Jack Shafer in *Slate* magazine, September 23, 2004

The *Factor* was in fact becoming more about Mr. O'Reilly than the issues. We were constantly being reminded that his books were on the *New York Times* bestseller list, or about the great column he had written for *WorldNet Daily,* or his radio program. He even periodically had a segment on his program where he would sit for a critique from Arthel Neville about his performance. Get it? It's all about Bill. I kept wishing she would say something honest like, "Bill, stop talking about yourself!"

—Alicia Colon in the *New York Sun,* September 17, 2004

It [fund-raiser for the State Theatre in Easton, Pennsylvania] was one of our fastest-selling shows. There have been times it takes nine months to sell [out] a show, but people really wanted to see Bill O'Reilly.

—Jamie Balliet, director of marketing at the State Theatre in the *Morning Call* (Allentown, Pennsylvania), January 8, 2003

He's overbearing. He interrupts and sneers at his guests. I enjoy that. . . . He's nasty and I don't agree with him. But it's entertaining.

—Victor Navasky, publisher of the *Nation,* in the *Fort Worth Star-Telegram,* July 17, 2003

So, Bill, I'm sorry to call
you one of the many people
who do lie, in my book.

—Al Franken in the *Kansas City Star*,
June 8, 2003, citing BookExpo America
in Los Angeles on May 31, 2003

[It] doesn't matter that he [O'Reilly] attacked us. We're big kids, we can take it. It's about attacking something that's working and good.

—George Clooney on the celebrity telethon *A Tribute to Heroes* and the *Concert for New York, E! News Daily,* November 8, 2001

*T*he *O'Reilly Factor* isn't really a talk show. It's an hour-long saloon argument.

—David Ruth, columnist, *Tampa Tribune,*
October 5, 2001

He's an empty-headed blowhard.

—*Washington Post* TV critic Tom Shales
in *People,* December 18, 2000

He likes to ask hard questions,
he interrupts too often and, since he
owns the microphone, he takes charge.
But it's not a newscast.

—Mike Wallace answering questions during his
acceptance of the Fred Friendly First Amendment Award
from Quinnipiac University on CNN.com, May 30, 2002

O'Reilly is no good at radio and part of that reason is because his most nuanced response to a complex question is "Shut up."

—G. Gordon Liddy, *Broadcasting and Cable,*
April 5, 2004, citing *Crossfire*

That wasn't nice, Bill. I didn't get old on purpose. It just happened. If you're lucky, it could happen to you.

—Andy Rooney, eighty-five, on O'Reilly discussing his age, *Pittsburgh Post-Gazette,* March 16, 2004

I don't want to make it personal, and Bill O'Reilly really has. He's gone after me and said I'm a smear artist. He has not pointed out one thing I've said that isn't true.

—Al Franken in the *New York Times,*
September 14, 2003